I0795277

SUPERSTARS

BILLIE EILISH

SINGING ★ SUPERSTAR

MEGAN BORGERT-SPANIOL

Big Buddy Books
An Imprint of Abdo Publishing
abdobooks.com

ABDOBOOKS.COM

Published by Abdo Publishing, a division of ABDO, PO Box 398166, Minneapolis, Minnesota 55439.
Copyright © 2022 by Abdo Consulting Group, Inc. International copyrights reserved in all countries. No part of this book may be reproduced in any form without written permission from the publisher.
Big Buddy Books™ is a trademark and logo of Abdo Publishing.
Printed in the United States of America, North Mankato, Minnesota

052021
092021

THIS BOOK CONTAINS RECYCLED MATERIALS

Design: Kelly Doudna, Mighty Media, Inc.
Production: Mighty Media, Inc.
Editor: Liz Salzmann
Cover Photograph: Evan Agostini/AP Images
Interior Photographs: Chris Pizzello/AP Images, pp. 25, 29 (bottom); Jordan Strauss/AP Images, p. 27; Flickr, pp. 7, 15, 28 (right); Picasa/Flickr, p. 11; Shutterstock Images, pp. 5, 9, 13, 17, 19, 21, 23, 29 (top); Sthanlee B. Mirador/AP Images, pp. 1, 28 (left)

Library of Congress Control Number: 2020949951

Publisher's Cataloging-in-Publication Data

Names: Borgert-Spaniol, Megan, author.
Title: Billie Eilish: singing superstar / by Megan Borgert-Spaniol
Other title: singing superstar
Description: Minneapolis, Minnesota : Abdo Publishing, 2022 | Series: Superstars | Includes online resources and index.
Identifiers: ISBN 9781532195662 (lib. bdg.) | ISBN 9781098216399 (ebook)
Subjects: LCSH: Eilish, Billie, 2001- --Juvenile literature. | Singers--United States--Biography--Juvenile literature. | Popular music--Juvenile literature. | Women singers--Juvenile literature. | Women--Biography--Juvenile literature.
Classification: DDC 782.42164--dc23

CONTENTS

Billie Eilish ★ 4
Family of Four ★ ★ ★ ★ ★ ★ ★ ★ ★ ★ ★ ★ ★ ★ ★ ★ ★ ★ ★ 6
Learning at Home ★ ★ ★ ★ ★ ★ ★ ★ ★ ★ ★ ★ ★ ★ ★ ★ ★ 8
Young Talent ★ 10
Rise to Fame ★ ★ ★ ★ ★ ★ ★ ★ ★ ★ ★ ★ ★ ★ ★ ★ ★ ★ ★ 14
Debut Album ★ ★ ★ ★ ★ ★ ★ ★ ★ ★ ★ ★ ★ ★ ★ ★ ★ ★ ★ 18
Family Support ★ ★ ★ ★ ★ ★ ★ ★ ★ ★ ★ ★ ★ ★ ★ ★ ★ ★ 22
Album of the Year ★ ★ ★ ★ ★ ★ ★ ★ ★ ★ ★ ★ ★ ★ ★ ★ ★ 24
Timeline ★ 28
Glossary ★ 30
Online Resources ★ ★ ★ ★ ★ ★ ★ ★ ★ ★ ★ ★ ★ ★ ★ ★ ★ 31
Index ★ 32

BILLIE EILISH

Billie Eilish is a singer and songwriter. Her music career took off in 2015. That's when a song she recorded went **viral**.

Billie brings her own voice and style to each of her songs. Her fans can't wait to hear what this music superstar will create next!

> "I just want to create stuff that people can feel. Fame is irrelevant."

A movie about Billie's life came out in February 2021. It is called *Billie Eilish: The World's a Little Blurry*.

FAMILY OF FOUR

Billie Eilish was born on December 18, 2001, in Los Angeles, California. Her full name is Billie Eilish Pirate Baird O'Connell.

Billie's parents are Maggie Baird and Patrick O'Connell. Both are actors. Billie has an older brother, Finneas.

SUPERSTAR ★ SCOOP

Billie was named after her grandfather, Bill Baird, who died before she was born. Her middle name, Pirate, was her brother's idea!

Billie and her family with Los Angeles mayor Eric Garcetti.
Left to right: Patrick, Maggie, Billie, Garcetti, Finneas

LEARNING AT HOME

Billie and Finneas were homeschooled. Their parents let them follow their creative interests. As a kid, Billie enjoyed dancing, horseback riding, and making costumes. She also liked to sing.

SUPERSTAR ★ SCOOP

Billie wrote her first song at age four. It was about falling into a black hole!

When she was 15, Billie took a test to earn her high school diploma.

YOUNG TALENT

When Billie was eight, she joined the Los Angeles Children's Chorus. She also began performing in talent shows.

Finneas was also interested in music. As a teenager, he wrote songs for his band. In 2015, Finneas asked Billie to sing one of his songs. It was called "Ocean Eyes."

The Los Angeles Children's Chorus met at the Pasadena Presbyterian Church in Pasadena, California.

Billie and Finneas recorded the song. Billie wanted to share it with her dance teacher. So, she and Finneas posted the song on the music website SoundCloud. The song went **viral**! It got 1,000 plays in one day.

SUPERSTAR ★ SCOOP

Five years after Billie posted it, "Ocean Eyes" had more than 40 million plays on SoundCloud!

Billie and Finneas often performed together.

RISE TO FAME

Music **producer** Justin Lubliner heard "Ocean Eyes." He asked Billie to work with his record **label**, Darkroom. She agreed. In 2016, Darkroom started producing Billie's music.

Billie's first **EP** came out in August 2017. It was called *Don't Smile at Me*. The next year, Billie went on tour. It was her Where's My Mind tour.

Billie's Where's My Mind tour included a show in Brussels, Belgium.

Billie's fans liked that her music sounded different. Many popular songs fit into **genres**. These include pop, rock, or **hip-hop**. But Billie's music didn't fit into any one genre.

Fans also liked Billie's songwriting. Many of her songs had dark themes. One example is "Bury a Friend." Billie said the song was **influenced** by her bad dreams.

> "I hate the idea of genres. I don't think a song should be put in a category."

Two of Billie's songs were featured on the hit Netflix TV show *13 Reasons Why*. Katherine Langford and Dylan Minnette were two of the show's stars.

DEBUT ALBUM

"Bury a Friend" is on Billie's 2019 album *When We All Fall Asleep, Where Do We Go?* The album was a success. Music magazine *Rolling Stone* ranked it the number one album of the year. In April 2019, Billie went on tour again.

SUPERSTAR ★ SCOOP

Billie liked to use **unsettling** images in her music videos. In one of them, she has real spiders crawling on her face!

Billie performed in Barcelona, Spain, during her When We All Fall Asleep tour.

In January 2020, Billie had more exciting news. She got to record the theme song for the 2021 James Bond movie, *No Time to Die*. Billie and Finneas wrote the song together.

Billie was now a big name in music. She was known for her soft singing voice. She was also known for her style. She liked to wear colorful, baggy clothes. She dyed her hair bright colors.

Daniel Craig stars as British secret agent James Bond in *No Time to Die*.

FAMILY SUPPORT

Billie enjoyed her quick rise to fame. But she also faced challenges, such as **depression**. Luckily, Billie's family was very supportive.

Finneas worked on songs with her. Her parents helped organize her shows. And Billie's mom made sure Billie had time to relax.

Billie appeared on the cover of the September/ October 2019 issue of *Popstar!* magazine.

ALBUM OF THE YEAR

January 2020 brought more excitement. *When We All Fall Asleep, Where Do We Go?* won Album of the Year at the Grammy Awards.

Billie also won Best New Artist, Song of the Year, and Record of the Year. She was the first woman to win these four Grammy awards in the same year.

Billie and Finneas holding their Grammy Award trophies.
At 18, Billie was the youngest person to win Album of the Year.

In March 2020, Billie started her Where Do We Go? tour. Billie played the first few shows. But then the **COVID-19 pandemic** struck. Billie had to **postpone** the remaining shows. Billie was sad she couldn't continue the tour.

But in November 2020, Billie got some good news. Her song "Everything I Wanted" received three **nominations** for the 2021 Grammy Awards. It won the Record of the Year award. Clearly, Billie would be an enduring superstar!

"I think the fans deserve everything. They're the only reason any of us are here at all."

At the 2021 Grammys, "Everything I Wanted" also won the Best Written Song for Visual Media award.

TIMELINE

2001
Billie Eilish was born on December 18 in Los Angeles, California.

2015
Billie's song "Ocean Eyes" went viral on the music sharing website SoundCloud.

2016
Billie started working with the record label Darkroom.

2017
Billie released the EP *Don't Smile at Me*.

2019

Billie released her album, *When We All Fall Asleep, Where Do We Go?*

MARCH 2020

Billie began her Where Do We Go? tour. She postponed most of the shows due to the COVID-19 pandemic.

2018

Billie went on her Where's My Mind tour.

JANUARY 2020

Billie won four major Grammy awards, including Album of the Year.

2021

Billie's song "Everything I Wanted" won two Grammy Awards. The James Bond movie *No Time to Die* was released. Its theme song was written and produced by Billie and Finneas.

GLOSSARY

COVID-19—a serious illness that first appeared in late 2019.

depression—a state of feeling sad or dejected.

EP—extended play. A recording that usually includes three to six songs.

genre (ZHAHN-ruh)—a type of art, music, or literature.

hip-hop—a form of popular music that features rhyme, spoken words, and electronic sounds. It is similar to rap music.

influence—to have an effect on something.

label—a company that produces musical recordings.

nomination—the state of being named as a possible winner.

pandemic—when a disease spreads very quickly over a large area.

postpone—to put off until a later time.

producer—a person who oversees the making of a movie, a play, an album, or a radio or TV show.

unsettling—likely to cause feelings such as fear, nervousness, or worry.

viral—quickly or widely spread, usually by electronic communication.

ONLINE RESOURCES

Booklinks
NONFICTION NETWORK
FREE! ONLINE NONFICTION RESOURCES

To learn more about Billie Eilish, please visit **abdobooklinks.com** or scan this QR code. These links are routinely monitored and updated to provide the most current information available.

INDEX

Belgium, 15
Billboard Music Awards, 27
Billie Eilish: The World's a Little Blurry, 5
birth, 6, 28

California, 6, 7, 10, 11, 28
childhood, 6, 8, 9, 10, 12
COVID-19 pandemic, 26, 27, 29
Craig, Daniel, 21

Darkroom, 14, 28
depression, 22
Don't Smile at Me, 14, 28

education, 8, 9

family, 6, 7, 8, 10, 12, 13, 20, 22, 25, 29

Garcetti, Eric, 7
Grammy Awards, 24, 25, 26, 29

Langford, Katherine, 17
Los Angeles Children's Chorus, 10, 11
Lubliner, Justin, 14

Minnette, Dylan, 17
movies, 5, 20, 21, 29

Netflix, 17
No Time to Die, 20, 21, 29

Pasadena Presbyterian Church, 11
performing, 10, 13, 14, 15, 18, 19, 26, 29
Popstar!, 23

Rolling Stone, 18

songwriting, 4, 8, 10, 16, 20, 29
SoundCloud, 12, 28
Spain, 19

13 Reasons Why, 17

When We All Fall Asleep, Where Do We Go?, 18, 24, 29